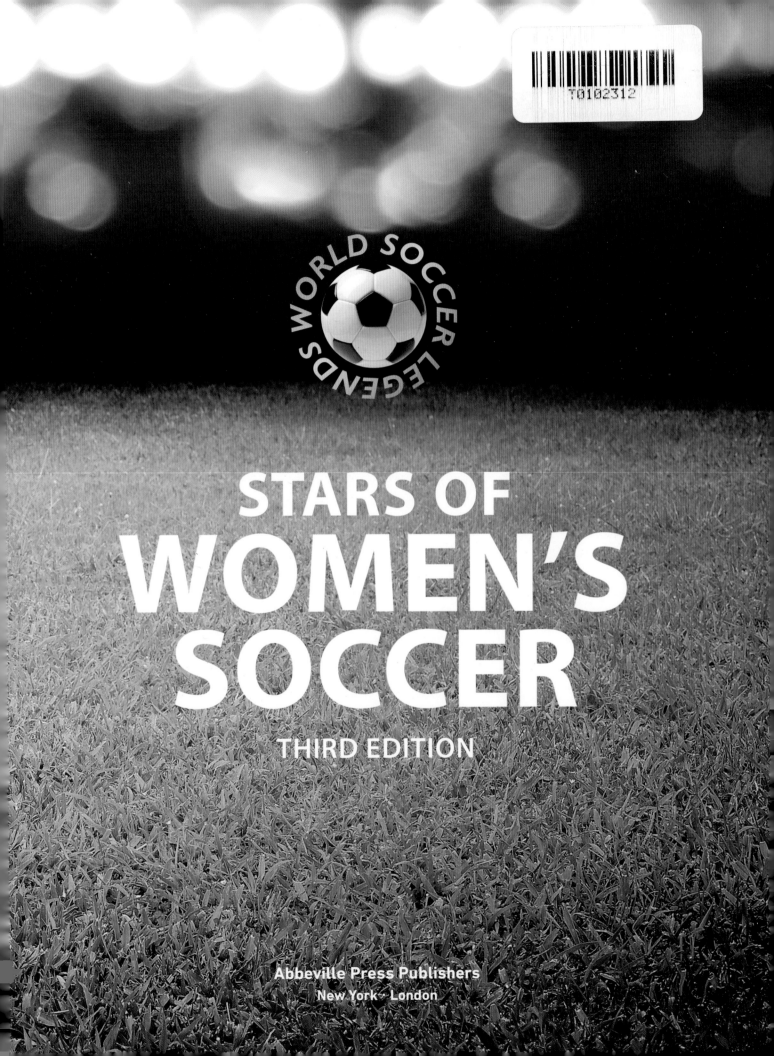

WORLD SOCCER LEGENDS

STARS OF
WOMEN'S
SOCCER

THIRD EDITION

Abbeville Press Publishers
New York · London

A portion of the book's proceeds are donated to the Hugo Bustamante AYSO Playership Fund, a national scholarship program to help ensure that no child misses the chance to play AYSO Soccer. Donations to the fund cover the cost of registration and a uniform for a child in need.

Statistics are current as of November 2020.

Text by Illugi Jökulsson
Design: THANK YOU
Layout: Árni Torfason

For the English-language edition
Project Editor: Lauren Bucca
Copy Editor: Ashley Benning
Layout: Ada Rodriguez
Production Manager: Louise Kurtz

PHOTOGRAPHY CREDITS

Getty Images: pp. 15 (Matthew Stockman), 20 (Kevin C. Cox), 30 (Rich Lam), 41 (Soccrates Images), 44 (Dean Mouhtaropoulos), 48–49 (Stuart Franklin-FIFA), 52 (Alex Grimm), 56 (Stanley Chou)

Megapixl: pp. 8 (© Katatonia82), 18 (© Mikeimagez), 22 (© Katatonia82), 34, 36 (© Katatonia82), 43 (© Zhukovsky), 54 (© Katatonia82)

Shutterstock: pp. 10 (Ververidis Vasilis), 12 (Jose Breton-Pics Action), 25 (Oleksandr Osipov), 26 (Jose Breton-Pics Action), 32 (Mikolaj Barbanell), 39 (Jose Breton-Pics Action), 46 (feelphoto), 50 (Mikolaj Barbanell), 58 (Jose Breton-Pics Action), 60 (lev radin), endpapers (Romain Biard)

Árni Torfason: pp. 1, 16

Wikipedia: p. 29 (Thewomensgame, CC-BY-4.0)

Third edition
10 9 8 7 6 5 4 3 2 1

ISBN 978-0-7892-1403-4

A previous edition of this book was cataloged as follows:
Library of Congress Cataloging-in-Publication Data
Illugi Jokulsson.
  Stars of women's soccer / by Illugi Jokulsson. —First edition.
  pages cm
  Audience: Age: 7.
  1. Women Soccer players—Biography—Juvenile literature. 2. Soccer for women—Juvenile literature.
I. Title.
  GV944.9.A1I55 2015
  796.334092'2--dc23
  [B]
  2015013479

For bulk and premium sales and for text adoption procedures, write to Customer Service Manager, Abbeville Press, 655 Third Avenue, New York, NY 10017, or call 1-800-ARTBOOK.

Visit Abbeville Press online at www.abbeville.com.

CONTENTS

SWEDEN

ASLLANI

KOSOVARE ASLLANI
FORWARD
SWEDEN
HEIGHT 5 FT 5 IN (165 CM)

BORN JULY 29, 1989
KRISTIANSTAD, SWEDEN

CURRENT TEAM:
REAL MADRID, SPAIN

INTERNATIONAL GAMES: 143
GOALS: 37

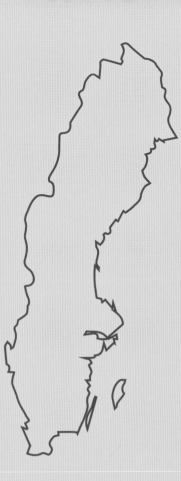

Asllani was born in the town of Kristianstad in South Sweden to Albanian Kosovar parents. Although she split her time between soccer and ice hockey growing up, soccer became her main focus. During her formative years as a player, she racked up goals for Linköpings FC in Sweden, and took a season off to broaden her horizons and play for the Chicago Red Stars. She later gave an impressive four-year performance at Paris Saint-Germain in the French capital, scoring freely, plus a year at Manchester City, but now she is a fixture on the first women's team of Spanish giant Real Madrid. Asllani has been a regular on the Swedish national team since 2008, although she was controversially left out of the squad for the 2011 World Cup. She played for Sweden at the 2016 Summer Olympics, where the team won a silver medal, and at the 2019 World Cup, where Sweden placed third. Asllani scored three goals at the World Cup, including her team's first goal of the tournament in the opening match against Chile. After taking a ball to the head toward the end of the semifinal, in the third place match against England she scored first again on the way to Sweden's 2–1 victory.

Asllani has a tattoo of a black double-headed eagle, symbolizing Albania, on her ankle. Nicknamed "Kosse," her first name is an obvious link to her Balkan heritage, while her status as a Balkan-Swedish soccer icon has drawn comparisons with men's soccer legend Zlatan Ibrahimović.

BRONZE

LUCY BRONZE
FULLBACK
ENGLAND
HEIGHT 5 FT 8 IN (172 CM)

BORN OCTOBER 28, 1991
IN BERWICK-UPON-TWEED,
ENGLAND

CURRENT TEAM:
MANCHESTER CITY, ENGLAND

INTERNATIONAL GAMES: 81
GOALS: 8

ENGLAND

Lucy Bronze began playing for Sunderland at the Under-12 academy level and signed a professional contract when she turned 16 in 2007. Only two years later she earned the Player of the Match award in the 2009 FA Women's Cup final against Arsenal, even with Arsenal besting Sunderland 2–1. The same year she shifted to collegiate play, joining the University of North Carolina Tar Heels in the United States and eventually becoming the first British player to win an NCAA Cup. However, she soon returned to England to resume her professional career, this time with Everton. She later moved to City rivals Liverpool, before heading to Manchester City and then to dominant French Olympique Lyonnais, where she became an integral part of an all-conquering team. Now Bronze finds herself back in England, with Manchester City again. With Bronze as a star player, the England national team took third place at the 2015 World Cup and made the semifinals in 2019. But although ultimate honors have eluded the national team, Bronze has gathered plenty of acclaim, being named to the FIFA Women's World Cup All-Star Squad in 2015, the FIFA FIFpro Women's World 11 in 2017 and 2019, as BBC Women's Footballer of the Year in 2018 and 2020, and winning the FIFA Women's World Cup Silver Ball in 2019. She is, quite simply, universally recognized as an elite player.

England head coach Phil Neville has utilized Bronze in midfield, seeing her as a complete player and a perfect fit for the role. "Playing Lucy in midfield . . . Pep Guardiola did it with Philip Lahm [at Bayern Munich], and he was voted one of the best rightbacks but he put him into midfield."

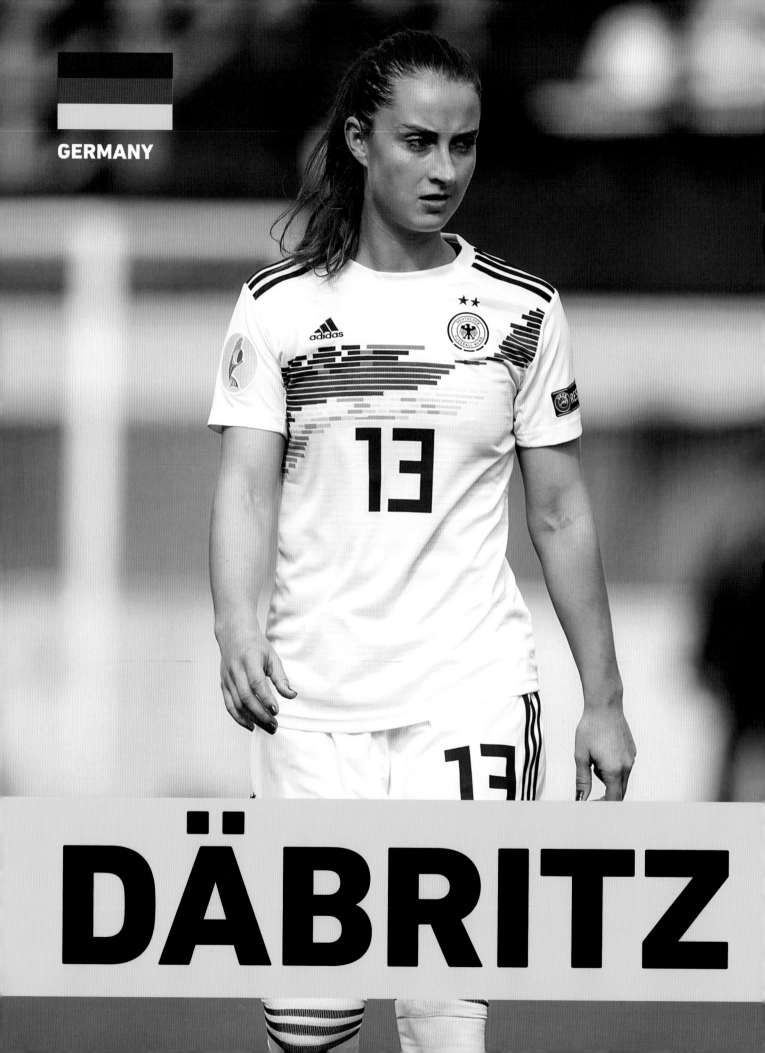

GERMANY

DÄBRITZ

SARA DÄBRITZ
MIDFIELDER
GERMANY
HEIGHT 5 FT 7 IN (170 CM)

BORN FEBRUARY 15, 1995
IN AMBERG, GERMANY

CURRENT TEAM:
PARIS SAINT-GERMAIN, FRANCE

INTERNATIONAL GAMES: 71
GOALS: 16

Germany's success at the 2016 Olympic Games in Rio de Janeiro, where the team took home the gold, was perhaps not so surprising given Germany's knack for assembling winning teams for both men's and women's soccer. However, the women's roster had seen a number of changes, and some pundits believed that Germany's performance might not be as seamless. For example, many were skeptical over coach Sylvia Neid's decision to play 21-year-old Sara Däbritz in midfield. It turned out that Däbritz fully lived up to Neid's expectations. Her performance was nearly immaculate, and the only time Germany lost was in a game where Däbritz was on the bench. She scored three important goals in the five games she played and was beaming with confidence the entire time, contributing both to the offense and defense, though it is apparent that Däbritz prefers shooting and passing.

The letter *ä* in her surname is pronounced with more of an "e" sound in German. Commit the name Sara Däbritz to memory—soccer fans will often hear it repeated in the decade to come as she makes her mark in midfield.

Däbritz was born and raised in the town Amberg in Bavaria, which is the southernmost and largest state in Germany. Bayern Münich is by far the most famous team there and supported by most residents of the region. The young Däbritz grew up surrounded by loyal Bayern fans and her deepest wish was to one day join the team. She began her career with Freiburg, but when she turned 20, Bayern finally came knocking. Däbritz is living proof that dreams can indeed come true.

CRYSTAL DUNN
FULLBACK
UNITED STATES
HEIGHT 5 FT 1 IN (155 CM)

BORN JULY 3, 1992
IN NEW HYDE PARK, NEW YORK, USA

CURRENT TEAM:
PORTLAND THORNS FC, UNITED STATES

INTERNATIONAL GAMES: 104
GOALS: 24

A native of Long Island, Crystal Dunn first made her name in soccer while attending the University of North Carolina at Chapel Hill, where she was named ACC Offensive Player of the Year in her senior year with the Tar Heels. After graduating, Dunn transferred to the capital's Washington Spirit, where she earned the 2015 NWSL Golden Boot and the league's Most Valuable Player award in her second season at the record young age of 23 with a chart-topping 15 goals. The diminutive fullback also boasted an amazing 0.77 goals-per-game average. Dunn has suggested that not making the 2015 World Cup team motivated her to excel.

She has since played in England for Chelsea, but returned home to sign with the North Carolina Courage. In October 2020, she transferred to the Portland Thorns, where she is expected to take a leading role. Dunn is an agile and lightning-quick player, with an unparalleled ability to bring a goal-scoring threat up from the rear, but has even played up front for her teams, such as the Courage. Wherever she is placed, Dunn will keep the team's play ticking and look to weigh in with goals of her own.

Dunn is no stranger to taking on issues off the soccer field. In 2016, on the eve of the Rio Olympics, she addressed issues such as racism and equal pay for female players in the docuseries *Keeping Score* with fellow U.S. teammates Hope Solo and Megan Rapinoe.

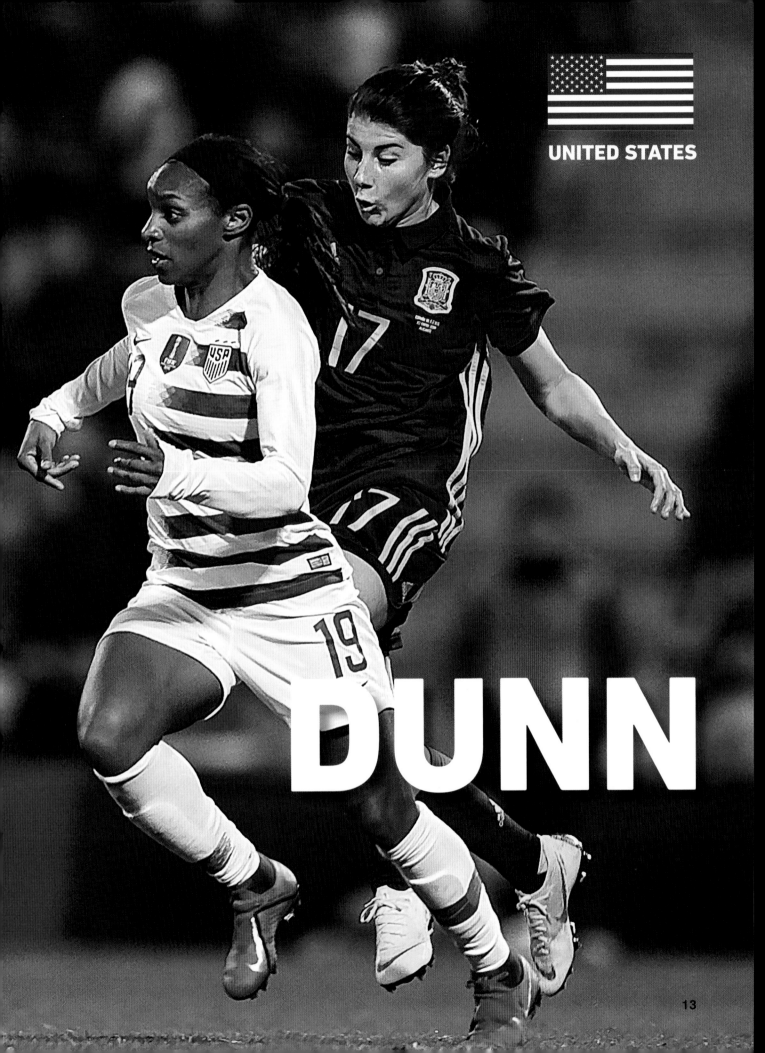

UNITED STATES

DUNN

13

JULIE ERTZ
MIDFIELDER, DEFENDER
UNITED STATES
HEIGHT 5 FT 7 IN (170 CM)

BORN APRIL 6, 1992
IN MESA, ARIZONA, USA

CURRENT TEAM:
CHICAGO RED STARS,
UNITED STATES

INTERNATIONAL GAMES: 102
GOALS: 20

Following her collegiate career with the Santa Clara University Broncos, when she was already a full international player, Julie Ertz signed with the Chicago Red Stars following the 2014 NWSL College Draft. She has built a stellar career in Chicago, being named US Soccer Female Player of the Year in 2017 and 2019, ahead of a raft of elite players. Her international progress has been spectacular, ever since Ertz captained Team USA to the Japan 2012 U20 FIFA Women's World Cup; winning the 2012 CONCACAF Under-20 Women's Championship along the way. Her participation in the 2015 and 2019 World Cup successes was then supplemented by the honor of being one of five U.S. players named in the FIFA FIFpro Women's World 11 in the memorable year of 2019. Furthermore, she was one of five nominees for the BBC Women's Footballer of the Year in 2020, ultimately coming in second behind England's Lucy Bronze. Ertz is a tough competitor on the field and loves to take control with her accurate tackling and insightful reading of the game. When she moved from central defense to a defensive midfield position for Team USA in the qualifying campaign that led to the 2019 World Cup, her influence grew, and she is poised to dominate midfield battles for years to come.

Julie and her sister Melanie Johnston played for the Sereno soccer team in Phoenix as teenagers. During her time there, the team won the state title no fewer than nine times, and Julie captained the team in the process.

ERTZ

ICELAND

GUNNARSDÓTTIR

SARA BJÖRK GUNNARSDÓTTIR
MIDFIELDER
ICELAND
HEIGHT 5 FT 8 IN (172 CM)

BORN SEPTEMBER 29, 1990
IN REYKJAVÍK, ICELAND

CURRENT TEAM:
OLYMPIQUE LYONNAIS, FRANCE

INTERNATIONAL GAMES: 134
GOALS: 20

Sara Björk Gunnarsdóttir's path to instant success with European top dog Lyon was a difficult one and continually forced the combative midfielder to learn from adversity. She decided to share her story in her book *Óstöðvandi* (*Unstoppable*). "For me it's about the struggles and setbacks that have made me who I am today," the 30-year-old explained to FIFA.com. "The character I am, how I play and how I am as a human. I had an injury for two years: a cruciate ligament rupture and a fractured thigh bone. Honestly, I didn't think I would play soccer again. It's about these setbacks, what I had to go through and how I got to the point where I am today . . . talk about anxiety in soccer, how the passion can affect you and how I handled it. At the end of the book I say that I'm really proud to be the person I am today because of my success, but mainly because of my setbacks and how I handled them." Her successes include being named Iceland's Woman Player of the Year six times. On the continent she has been part of winning teams for the Swedish league (FC Rosengård four times) and the German league (VfL Wolfsburg league and cup doubles three times).

In one of the oddities to come out of the coronavirus pandemic, Gunnarsdóttir has earned a unique accolade: Because of the extended season, after winning the German League and Cup with Wolfsburg, she was able to turn around and win against them in the Women's Champions League final with Olympique Lyonnais.

HARDER

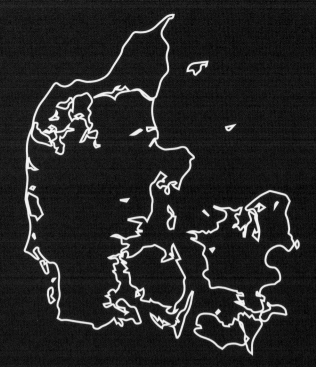

PERNILLE HARDER
FORWARD
DENMARK
HEIGHT 5 FT 7 IN (170 CM)

BORN NOVEMBER 15, 1992
IN IKAST, DENMARK

CURRENT TEAM:
CHELSEA, ENGLAND

INTERNATIONAL GAMES: 122
GOALS: 64

Pernille Harder grew up in the quiet environs of the Danish Jutland region, but has risen to the top of world soccer. Harder is a versatile player capable of making an impact in multiple positions, but she might be best described as a 10—an attacking player who has great technique and is involved in any forward buildup. Harder is a creative and intelligent second forward who relies on great positioning, and intricate passing and shooting, to make her mark. For the German team Wolfsburg, she mainly operated as a forward and second forward in a 4-4-2 formation and as an attacking midfielder in a 4-2-3-1 formation. She played for three seasons in Germany at the summit of the European teams and averaged almost a goal per game, winning league and cup honors domestically but continually coming in second to French powerhouse Lyon internationally. Earlier in her career, she had been a goal machine for Swedish team Linköpings FC, leading the team to league and cup successes. In 2017, the year she joined Wolfsburg, she captained the Danish team to the final of the UEFA Women's Euro 2017 and scored a goal in Denmark's 4—2 defeat by the Netherlands. She was voted runner-up to Lieke Martens in the UEFA Women's Player of the Year Award for 2016–17.

On September 1, 2020, Harder signed a three-year contract with England's Chelsea for a world-record fee for a female soccer player, reportedly somewhere in the region of $400,000. Personal factors didn't pose a problem—Harder's partner, Magdalena Eriksson of Sweden, is Chelsea's captain!

UNITED STATES

HEATH

20

TOBIN HEATH

MIDFIELDER
UNITED STATES
HEIGHT 5 FT 6 IN (167 CM)

BORN MAY 29, 1988
IN BASKING RIDGE, NEW JERSEY, USA

CURRENT TEAM:
MANCHESTER UNITED, ENGLAND

INTERNATIONAL GAMES: 168
GOALS: 33

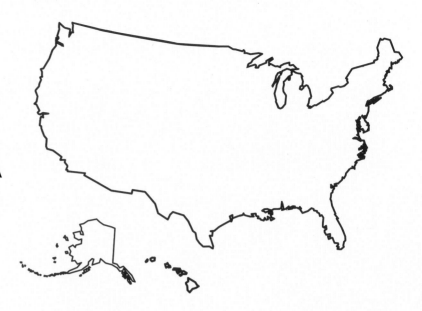

Despite Tobin Heath's ability to score goals while under great pressure, her primary role is to drive midfield play and create opportunities for her attacking teammates. And she certainly delivers—and then some! She is one of Team USA's most ingenious midfielders and her reputation has circled the globe. When she played with Paris Saint-Germain in 2013–14, she was the team's best player—an impressive feat, given that the ranks of PSG do not lack for legends. Heath is a soccer player to the bone and when she played with the University of North Carolina Tar Heels, her teammates claimed that "she would find her way to a soccer field morning, noon, and night." In 2016, Heath was named U.S. Soccer Female Player of the Year, an honor voted on by soccer coaches, players, administrators, and media. This multitalented woman is also the creative director of the luxury lifestyle brand Re—inc, a joint project with former Team USA teammates Christen Press, Meghan Klingenberg, and Megan Rapinoe to "reimagine the status quo."

In 2016, Heath was chosen Soccer Female Player of the Year by the US Soccer Federation. The nomination was phrased in flattering words to say the least: "She has always been one of the USA's most skillful players. She has long dazzled fans with her keen passing and dynamic dribbling, and she creates excitement on whichever flank she happens to occupy, causing nightmares for opposing defenders with her combination of speed, fitness, and soccer savvy."

HEGERBERG

ADA HEGERBERG
FORWARD
NORWAY
HEIGHT 5 FT 10 IN (178 CM)

BORN JULY 10, 1995
IN MOLDE, NORWAY

CURRENT TEAM:
OLYMPIQUE LYONNAIS, FRANCE

INTERNATIONAL GAMES: 66
GOALS: 38

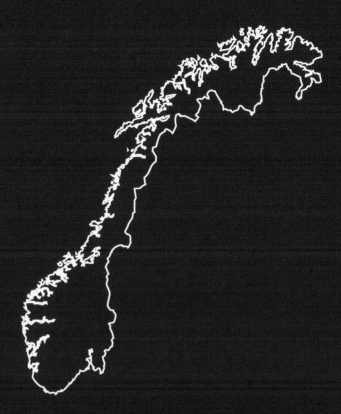

Since making her debut as a top-level soccer player with Norway's Kolbotn in 2010, at the tender age of 15, Ada Martine Stolsmo Hegerberg has scored goals by the bucketful wherever she has played. Her breakthrough was in the summer of 2014, when she transferred to Olympique Lyonnais. Her record there is jaw-dropping, her goal totals far exceeding the number of games played. Of course, her trophy haul at the French giant reflects this. In the 2015–16 season, she was selected UEFA Best Women's Player in Europe. She was also The 100 Best Female Soccer Players in the World leader in 2016. In 2017, she was named the BBC Women's Footballer of the Year (which she would receive again in 2019). However, Hegerberg's league play success continued: On December 3, 2018, she received the very first Ballon d'Or Féminin, the ultimate individual accolade in women's soccer. Unfortunately, the Norwegian national team has not been able to share in her successes. In the summer of 2017, Hegerberg decided to stop representing the national team as part of a dispute with the Norwegian Football Federation about its treatment of women's soccer. And she extended her protest to the 2019 World Cup when she felt the interim improvements did not go far enough to level the playing field.

For a tall forward, Hegerberg has proven to be very adept at ball handling and lithe footwork. Her dribbling skills allow her to drift around defenders and maximize scoring opportunities. Going up against her one-on-one is a real challenge.

AMANDINE HENRY
DEFENSIVE MIDFIELDER
FRANCE
HEIGHT 5 FT 7 IN (170 CM)

BORN SEPTEMBER 28, 1989
LILLE, FRANCE

CURRENT TEAM:
OLYMPIQUE LYONNAIS, FRANCE

INTERNATIONAL GAMES: 92
GOALS: 13

Amandine Henry's head coach at the Portland Thorns, where she played for a season before heading back to continue collecting trophies with Lyon, describes her in vivid terms as a complete midfield player: "She can go box to box. She can break up plays. She can pass. She can shoot. She communicates. She organizes. She's a midfield general who adds a percentage to every player who's around her. Incredibly intelligent, smart, and creative, and makes things look very easy." In short, Henry has no weaknesses as a player. She is the fulcrum, the brain, and the beating heart of an Olympique Lyonnais team which is still on an unparalleled run of success. At the 2015 World Cup, where France was unlucky to lose to Germany on penalties in the quarterfinals, she distinguished herself by winning the Silver Ball and making the FIFA All-Star Team. Henry was determined to lead France to glory on home soil in the 2019 World Cup, but France again dropped out in the quarterfinals, this time losing 2–1 to eventual winners Team USA. Time will tell if Henry is destined for more awards with the French team, but she will be eager to add international honors to her huge haul of team trophies. Don't bet against France at the next Euro!

Each year, Mattel, the maker of Barbie dolls, elects an outstanding woman to celebrate. In 2020, Henry was chosen as someone who achieves regardless of stereotypes and who is a great role model. Henry is also a published author, having written a children's book called *Croire en ses rêves! (Believe in Your Dreams!)*.

HENRY

ENGLAND

HOUGHTON

26

STEPH HOUGHTON
CENTRAL DEFENDER
ENGLAND
HEIGHT 5 FT 9 IN (175 CM)

BORN APRIL 23, 1988
IN DURHAM, ENGLAND

CURRENT TEAM:
MANCHESTER CITY, ENGLAND

INTERNATIONAL GAMES: 120
GOALS: 11

Stephanie Jayne Houghton grew up in South Hetton in County Durham, in the northeast of England. It's an area with an active soccer culture, and Houghton started playing the sport in elementary school, first on the playground and then going on to get a midfielder spot on the official intermural team with the boys. She describes her childhood playing days to the BBC as a formative experience: "Playing with the boys made me a better soccer player, it made me more competitive and made me want to win even more. You were playing against the boys and wanted to prove how good you were." And that competitive streak has served her well on for the English national team, for which she first played in 2007. Although injuries sidelined her for the 2007 World Cup and Euro 2009, she was back on the field in the 2011 World Cup and Euro 2013. She became England's captain in January 2014. A champion in league play for Arsenal and Manchester City, Houghton was also pivotal in Great Britain's showing during the group stage at the 2012 London Olympics, scoring in all three wins.

Houghton raised eyebrows with her answer to Jamie Carragher's question on The Greatest Game podcast: "To be honest, even though I'm in the women's game, I don't really watch a lot of women's soccer." It should be pointed out that many of the games in the top women's leagues take place while she is busy playing!

SAM KERR
FORWARD
AUSTRALIA
HEIGHT 5 FT 6 IN (167 CM)

BORN SEPTEMBER 10, 1993
IN EAST FREMANTLE, AUSTRALIA

CURRENT TEAM: CHELSEA, ENGLAND

INTERNATIONAL GAMES: 88
GOALS: 42

The 27-year-old captain of Matildas—the Australia women's national soccer team—comes from a soccer family. Her father and uncles were pro-soccer players in the West Australian Football League. Following in the family tradition she joined the Matildas at age 15. The year 2019 was a big one for her: She scored five goals in the World Cup and was in the running for both the Best Women's Player at the FIFA Soccer Awards and the Ballon d'Or, losing out to Megan Rapinoe. Kerr is the first Australian (male or female) to score a hat trick at a World Cup and was named the 2017 Asian Football Confederation's Women's Player of the Year and received the awards for Best International Women's Soccer Player and the Best Player in the NWSL at the 2019 ESPY Awards. According to the *Guardian*'s annual list for 2019, she is the best female player on the planet. Kerr's playing style is predicated on her movement and positioning in the final third. She is a complete forward who recognizes opportunities to advance possessions forward by dropping deep, bringing teammates into play, or running the channels. At the front of the pack on the field, Kerr sets the pace of play taking long balls, linking up play, breaking lines, and always pushing the advantage.

Kerr is excellent at reading a game and can apply this skill to elevate her teammates. This connection was particularly strong with Yuki Nagasato when they were on the Red Stars together. The Japanese player's stats were her strongest ever when the two were collaborating on the field in 2019.

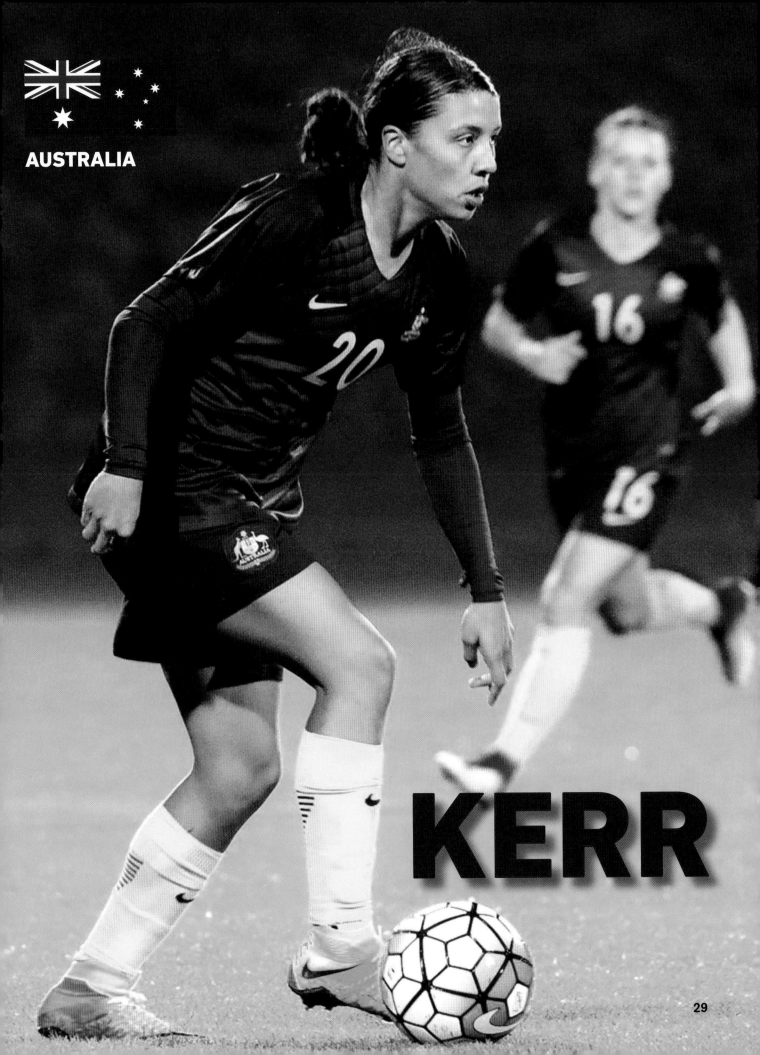

AUSTRALIA

KERR

29

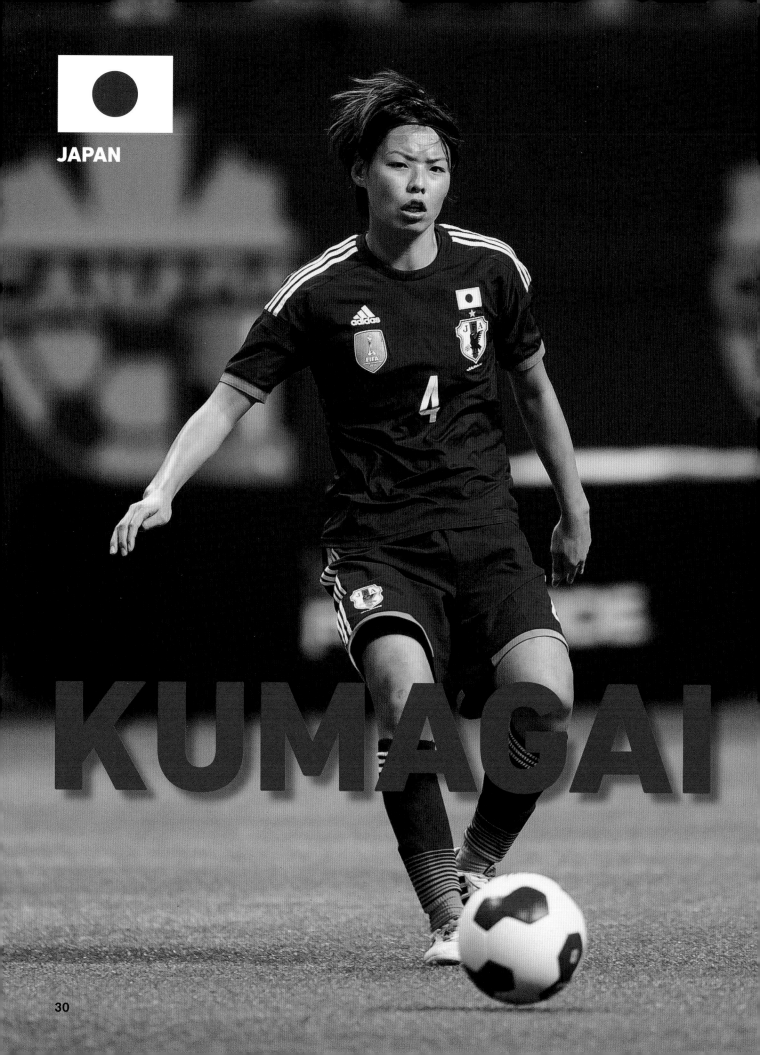

JAPAN

KUMAGAI

30

SAKI KUMAGAI
DEFENDER
JAPAN
HEIGHT 5 FT 8 IN (173 CM)

BORN OCTOBER 17, 1990
IN SAPPORO, JAPAN

CURRENT TEAM:
OLYMPIQUE LYONNAIS, FRANCE

INTERNATIONAL GAMES: 112
GOALS: 1

Saki Kumagai has gained recognition as a leading Asian player regardless of gender. Her icy calm during crucial plays and concentration even off-the-ball are what have made her a key part of Olympique Lyonnais's rise to dominance. She joined the French powerhouse in 2013, transferring from Frankfurt. Before that she played with the Uzawa Red Diamonds of Saitama in Japan. The Sapporo native has also had a stellar history in World Cup play. In the 2011 World Cup final penalty shootout against Team USA, it was Kumagai who scored to take Japan to the top for the first time. Japan's 2015 run, coming in second to the U.S. team, showed the nation was still to be reckoned with. In 2019 Kumagai captained a young group of Nadeshiko League Japanese players during the 2019 World Cup in France. Coach Asako Takakura's team included only three other players with records near Kumagai's 108 national caps, so the pressure was on. When Japan was knocked out in the Round of 16, Kumagai's surge of emotion drew her Dutch opponents to immediately console the competitive defender.

At 30 years old, Kumagai has earned accolades as an Olympic silver medalist, FIFA World Cup winner, and Asian Cup champion as well as being a four-time UEFA Champions League winner and six-time league champion with Olympique Lyonnais. She was nominated as the 2019 BBC Women's Footballer of the Year, but was bested in the final vote by her Lyon teammate Ada Hegerberg.

"It's quite difficult to compare the last three World Cups—the one we won, the one as runners-up, and the last one. The last one, we had a very young team with inexperienced players. It cost us as a team, but gaining the experience we had will make us a better team over the next few years," Kumagai said after receiving her AFC Player of the Year 2019 award in Hong Kong.

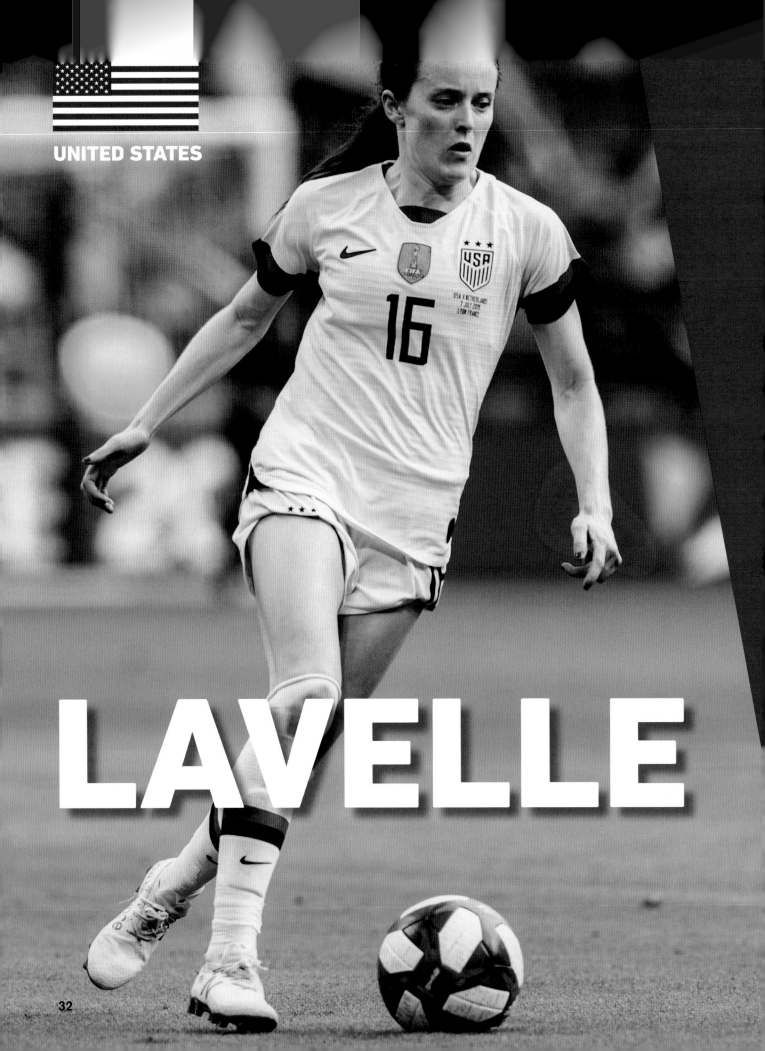

LAVELLE

ROSE LAVELLE
MIDFIELDER
UNITED STATES
HEIGHT 5 FT 4 IN (162 CM)

BORN MAY 14, 1995
IN CINCINNATI, OHIO, USA

CURRENT TEAM:
MANCHESTER CITY, ENGLAND

INTERNATIONAL GAMES: 45
GOALS: 12

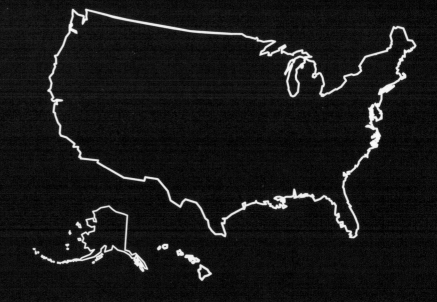

Breaking through as a collegiate player, Rose Lavelle starred for the University of Wisconsin-Madison and was named Big Ten Conference Freshman of the Year when the Badgers won the Big Ten Women's Soccer Tournament in 2014. Lavelle was named first-team All-American by the National Soccer Coaches Association of America in 2015 and Big Ten Midfielder of the Year consecutively in 2015 and 2016. After honing her craft with a succession of American teams, where her career was hampered by a series of troublesome injuries, Lavelle has now taken the leap overseas to captain midfield operations for Manchester City in England. Lavelle's small frame belies a ruthlessness and a fierce competitive streak, but her most outstanding attributes have to be her technical skill and flair. She has the ability to glide past opponents in a crowded midfield, always with an eye for sending her teammates an inch-perfect pass—or going for the goal herself, such as the second score in a 2–0 final win against the Netherlands at the 2019 World Cup. After that tournament, Lavelle was named sixth of the world's top 11 players by The Best FIFA Football Awards 2019, and was chosen as one of the world's top three midfielders by her professional peers in the 2019 FIFA FIFPro World XI.

Following Lavelle's arrival at Manchester City in August 2020, the "Manchester Derby" has taken on a distinctly American hue. While Lavelle joined international teammate Sam Mewis in the blue half of Manchester, their red rivals at Manchester United have Tobin Heath and Christen Press to call upon.

LE SOMMER

EUGÉNIE LE SOMMER
FORWARD/ATTACKING MIDFIELDER
FRANCE
HEIGHT 5 FT 3 IN (160 CM)

BORN MAY 18, 1989
IN GRASSE, FRANCE

CURRENT TEAM:
OLYMPIQUE LYONNAIS, FRANCE

INTERNATIONAL GAMES: 174
GOALS: 86

In good company with Wendie Renard and midfielders Louisa Nécib and Camille Abily, forward Eugénie Le Sommer represents the great advancement and recent successes of both the French league champions Lyon and the magnificent French national team. She was only 19 years old when she played her first game with the national team and a year later she left Stade Briochin to join the ranks of Lyon. In a decade representing Olympique Lyonnais, she has truly blossomed as a well-rounded soccer player and gathered a host of titles, and now it's only a matter of time until the French team snatches the title at a major tournament, either at the World Cup or the upcoming European Championship.

Le Sommer's gifts are on full display in her confident ball control as well as her particular flair for weaving through the thick of opponents' defenses. In fact, Le Sommer is an all-around player and scores goals of every kind. In 2017, she had played in nearly 240 games and scored 215 goals, almost a goal per game, the statistics of a soccer superstar. On September 22, 2020, Le Sommer's two goals in France's win over North Macedonia in a Euro 2021 qualifier gave her the lead as the all-time top scorer for Les Bleues, besting by one point Marinette Pichon's previous record of 81 goals.

Le Sommer can play as effectively as a striker (a 9), a "false 9" or traditional offensive midfielder, or a 10, an attacking playmaker. The role of the false 9 is to create problems for the opposing center backs and/or fill the space left open in the pursuit of the "real 9" in order to pass, create opportunities, or shoot.

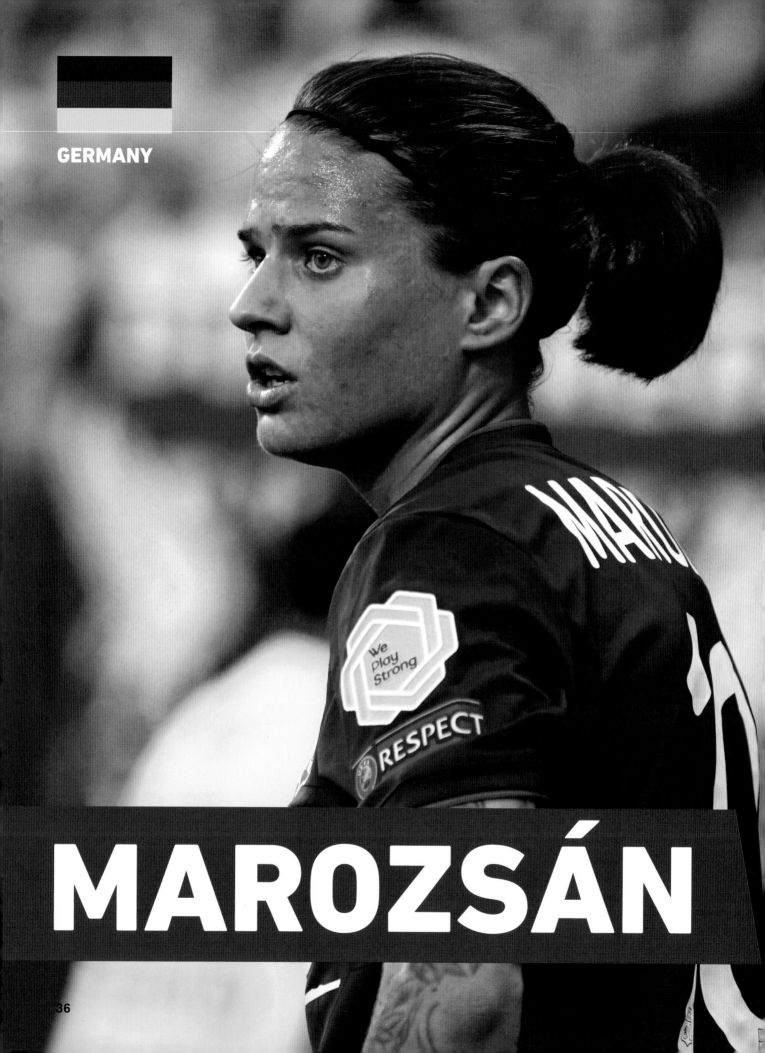

MAROZSÁN

DZSENIFER MAROZSÁN

MIDFIELDER
GERMANY
HEIGHT 5 FT 7 IN (170 CM)

BORN APRIL 18, 1992
IN BUDAPEST, HUNGARY

CURRENT TEAM:
OLYMPIQUE LYONNAIS, FRANCE

INTERNATIONAL GAMES: 100
GOALS: 33

The German women's national team was nearly unstoppable over the first decade of the 21st century. They won the world championship title both in 2004 and 2007. The magnificent Birgit Prinz covered the front lines at the time and the sturdy Nadine Angerer stood guard in the goal. Germany was also invincible in the Euros with six consecutive tournament victories 1995–2013. Now after a bumpy period, the German team is building a fresh and stronger than ever group, led by the new captain Dzsenifer Marozsán. The Germans trust that she will steer an exciting team composed of both newcomers and veterans back onto the road to victory. Germany's performance during the 2016 Olympic Games in Rio is surely an indicator of new times, with Marozsán scoring one of two goals in Germany's 2–1 victory over Sweden.

Marozsán was actually born in Hungary but moved to Germany, where her father played soccer, at a very young age. The fact that Marozsán was made captain at such a young age shows that she is a natural-born leader. Germany's previous captains have usually been more experienced players. Still, Marozsán's skillfulness in the sport is inarguable. She brilliantly conducts the offense but also springs through the defense and racks up countless goals. Something spectacular always happens when Dzenifer Marozsán is on the ball!

In 2017, Marozsán became the youngest player to have participated in Germany's Bundesliga. She was then 14 years and seven months old. She also holds the record as the youngest goal scorer, at the age of 15 years and 4 months.

LIEKE MARTENS
MIDFIELDER
NETHERLANDS
HEIGHT 5 FT 7 IN (170 CM)

BORN DECEMBER 16, 1992
IN BERGEN, THE NETHERLANDS

CURRENT TEAM:
FC BARCELONA, SPAIN

INTERNATIONAL GAMES: 116
GOALS: 46

The Dutch women's national team played their first game in 1971 and suffered a humiliating defeat at the hands of France. Over the next 40 years, they were unfortunately an easy prey for other stronger European teams and never made it to any major tournament. But then something miraculous happened. Not only did the Netherlands manage to qualify for the 2015 World Cup in Canada and perform there beyond the wildest expectations of fans by fighting their way to the knockout phase, but the team then went on to conquer in the 2017 Euro. No one imagined that the Dutch host team would be as strong or triumphant as they turned out to be. The title was absolutely deserved, made manifest by an incredible performance. As the team continues its upward climb, one of its players—the incredibly talented and promising Lieke Martens—has already leapt to the highest level of players. Martens has participated in over 100 international games, and counting, scoring a goal in every second or third game on average. She is quick as a flash, incredibly agile and cunning, and fearlessly dashes into every attack. Although the Netherlands had to make do with silver medals at the 2019 World Cup, Martens is still at the top of her game and could easily drive the team to glory in the next major tournaments, either the Euro or the World Cup itself. Watch this space!

The 2017 Euro Final was a pure delight to watch. The Netherlands faced Denmark, whose strong performance had come as a surprise when they managed to eliminate the powerful Germans. The Danes scored a goal and were ahead, but Miedema leveled the score and Martens then swept in and scored another goal, giving the Netherlands the lead. The final score was 4–2 for the Netherlands, and Martens received the UEFA Women's Player of the Year Award.

MARTENS

VIVIANNE MIEDEMA
FORWARD
THE NETHERLANDS
HEIGHT 5 FT 9 IN (175 CM)

BORN JULY 15, 1996
IN HOOGEVEEN, THE NETHERLANDS

CURRENT TEAM:
ARSENAL, ENGLAND

INTERNATIONAL GAMES: 91
GOALS: 70

Anna Margaretha Marina Astrid ("Vivi-anne") Miedema, to give her breathtak-ingly long full name, started her soccer career at the age of 14 in SC Heeren-veen, thus becoming the youngest player ever in the professional women's soccer league in the Netherlands. Her record for Heerenveen has the rare distinction of more goals scored than games played! In June 2014, when she was still only 17, Miedema signed with Bayern Munich of Germany, where she was compared to her illustrious coun-tryman Arjen Robben. In May 2017, she moved to London giant Arse-nal, where she is so far repeating her mind-boggling performance scoring more than a goal per game.

In 2013, coach Roger Reijners gave Miedema her first slot on the senior Netherlands women's national soccer team. For the U-19 team, Miedema was instrumental in winning the 2014 European Championship, followed by a triumphant European Championship campaign in 2017 with the senior team and second place at the 2019 World Cup. Miedema is a complete forward who can score goals with either foot, as well as with her head. She combines a physical presence with very clever movement and a clinical finishing edge in front of the goal—at times she can be unstoppable for the defender unlucky enough to be tasked with guarding her. And she is only getting better.

Miedema has claimed that she only focuses on her team's success, not on scoring goals herself. However, at the tender age of 24, she is already the highest-scoring Dutch international player in history—male or female. With legends such as Marco Van Basten in her rearview mirror, the sky is the limit for Miedema.

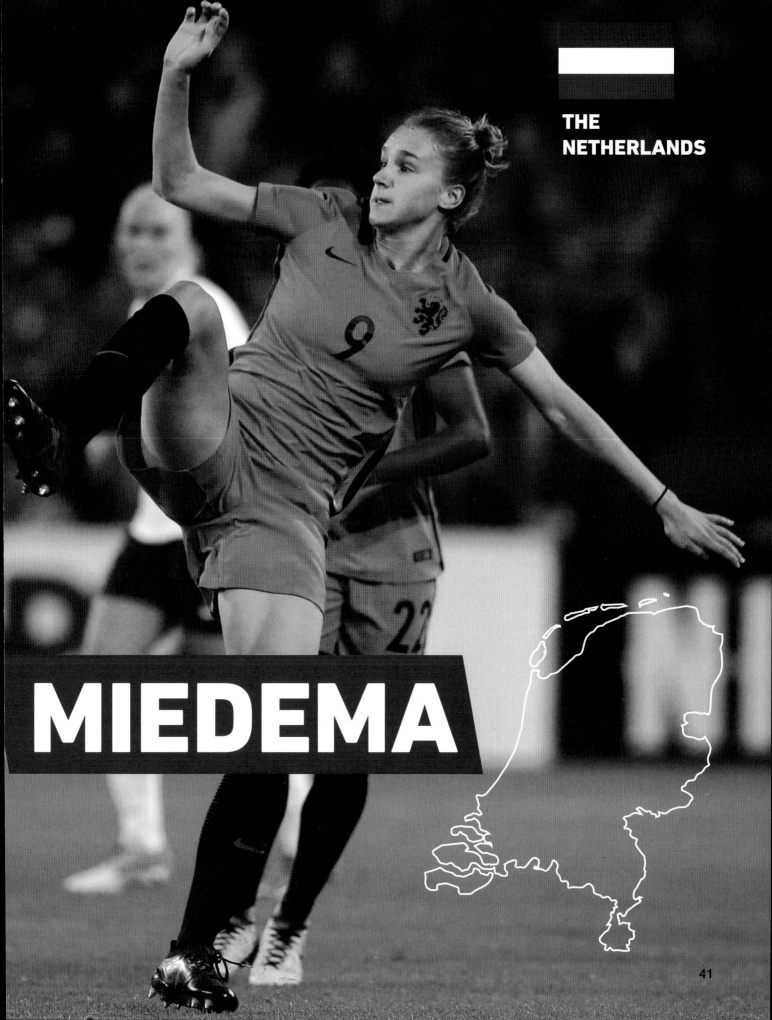

THE
NETHERLANDS

MIEDEMA

ALEX MORGAN
FORWARD
UNITED STATES
HEIGHT 5 FT 7 IN (170 CM)

BORN JULY 2, 1989
SAN DIMAS, CALIFORNIA, USA

CURRENT TEAM:
TOTTENHAM HOTSPUR, ENGLAND

INTERNATIONAL GAMES: 169
GOALS: 107

Alex Morgan is a defender's worst nightmare. She is a predatory attacker with sharp scoring instincts, which she acts on with great speed and strength. But it's not all about her; whenever a teammate is in a better position, she will find her with a pass to optimize scoring opportunities. Morgan was already a star at the college level with the California Golden Bears of UC Berkeley, which she led in scoring and helped the team reach the NCAA Tournament four years in a row. She was the youngest member of the US national team that placed second at the 2011 Women's World Cup, where she scored in the final against Japan. Morgan became an American hero a year later at the Summer Olympics in London. She secured her team a place in the final by scoring the winning goal against Canada in extra time and went on to assist Carli Lloyd twice in the final game to secure the gold. Since then, Morgan has gone from strength to strength, as one of the cocaptains of Team USA in back-to-back World Cup wins in 2015 and 2019. In 2019 Morgan took the tournament's Silver Boot, losing out to Megan Rapinoe for the Gold only through a tiebreaker of who had scored her six goals in the fewest minutes.

MORGAN

UNITED STATES

Eyebrows raised when Morgan celebrated scoring the decisive goal in Team USA's 2–1 semifinal victory against England at the 2019 World Cup by miming sipping a cup of tea. Some perceived it as a jab at her opponents, while others saw it as merely a storm in a teacup!

DENMARK

NADIM

NADIA NADIM
FORWARD
DENMARK
HEIGHT 5 FT 9 IN (175 CM)

BORN JANUARY 2, 1988
IN HERAT, AFGHANISTAN

CURRENT TEAM:
PARIS SAINT-GERMAIN, FRANCE

INTERNATIONAL GAMES: 97
GOALS: 38

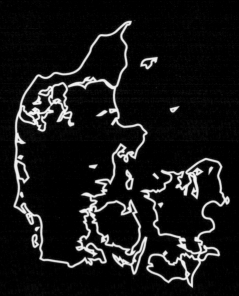

Nadia Nadim is an interesting example of how sports, positivity, and determination can overcome all obstacles. Nadim was born in worn-torn Afghanistan where her father, a general in the Afghan army, was killed by Taliban extremists. At 12 years old, her life was already in danger. Under Taliban rule, girls were forbidden to educate themselves, let alone play soccer. Nadim and her family fled the country and prayed for the best, and eventually they stepped out of the back of a truck as refugees in faraway Denmark. And there Nadim has flourished.

Nadim has traveled widely as a daring and insightful forward—playing for Sky Blue in New Jersey in 2014–15, scoring 13 goals in 24 games. She then joined the Portland Thorns in the company of legends such as Canadian Christine Sinclair and Team USA players Lindsey Horan, Meghan Klingenberg, and Tobin Heath. In 2016, Nadim became the team's top goal scorer. She scored a total of 15 goals for Portland in 37 games. Wherever Nadim plays she spreads her positive spirit, always attracting attention for her skill and optimism. She played a big role in Denmark's success at the 2017 Euro, scoring in an unexpected victory over Germany, and in the final against the Netherlands, though it wasn't enough to secure the title.

Nadia Nadim lived in a refugee camp in Denmark for a long time. She is the perfect example of the ways in which refugees can contribute to the countries that shelter them. She intends to become a doctor after she retires from soccer so she can travel the world and assist people who need help. And she's well-prepared for the task, speaking nine languages fluently: Danish, English, German, Persian, Urdu, Dari, Hindi, Arabic, and French!

O'HARA

KELLEY O'HARA
FULLBACK / WINGER
UNITED STATES
HEIGHT 5 FT 5 IN (165 CM)

BORN AUGUST 4, 1988
IN FAYETTEVILLE, GEORGIA, USA

CURRENT TEAM:
UTAH ROYALS FC, UNITED STATES

INTERNATIONAL GAMES: 131
GOALS: 2

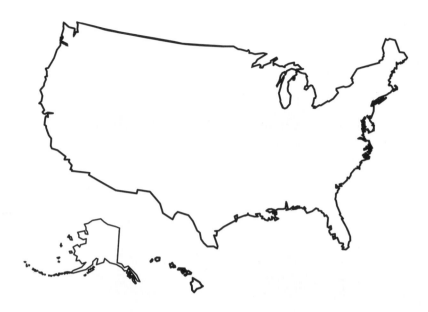

Kelley O'Hara is the consummate team player. She doesn't care where she is told to go on the soccer field—at fullback, on the wing, or up front—all she wants to do is leave everything on the field so that her team can win. Her selflessness has led her from putting in endless hours as a junior prospect in her native Georgia to the world's elite, O'Hara tasted success early in her career, winning a WPS Championship in 2010 with FC Gold Pride of Santa Clara, California. In the same year, she started an international career which has seen her become one of the most decorated players today, with an Olympic gold medal (she was one of three players on the national team who played every minute for the United States in the 2012 Olympic Games) and two World Cups at the center of her trophy haul. In addition, she was recognized in the FIFA FIFpro Women's Team of the Year in 2019. However, she also has interests outside the world of soccer, and in July 2020, she launched a podcast with website Just Women's Sports. O'Hara had been asked to join the advisory board, but instead requested to host their podcast, with the goal of generating "open, candid conversations" about the lives of athletes, particularly female athletes.

O'Hara turned heads after the 2019 World Cup final when, like many male athletes before her, she ran to the stands to receive a kiss from her girlfriend. Unlike a handful of her teammates, O'Hara was not publicly out until that moment of celebration.

ALEXANDRA POPP
FORWARD/ATTACKING MIDFIELDER
GERMANY
HEIGHT 5 FT 9 IN (175 CM)

BORN APRIL 6, 1991
IN WITTEN, GERMANY

CURRENT TEAM:
WOLFSBURG, GERMANY

INTERNATIONAL GAMES: 108
GOALS: 53

Two of the greatest goal scorers on Germany's powerful national team both retired between 2015 and 2017, namely, Célia Šašić and Anja Mittag. That left even more responsibility on Alexandra Popp's shoulders, who has in fact played for the national team since 2010, debuting at only 19 years old to great success. So now the pressure is on Popp to rack up the goals on behalf of the team, which is fortunate for Germany, because she is clearly reaching the zenith of her soccer career as a goal-scoring machine. Popp first stepped on the world stage when she played for the U-20 German national team at the 2010 World Cup. Germany won the tourna-ment with a marvelous team, in which Dzenifer Marozsán burst forth as a fully rounded player, but no one performed better than Popp. She scored in every game, with a total of 10 goals in six games. Popp has also amassed a host of accolades with Wolfsburg in the Bundesliga, becoming league champion five times and twice winning the Champions League title. Germany's siege on national team honors in the next few years will largely depend on the performance of this versatile and dynamic forward. And with Popp, there is no lack of will: "I want to give absolutely everything I can for the team!"

Popp has already begun to prepare for life beyond soccer. She is a qualified zookeeper and works at a zoo in the town of Lehre: "All the animals we have are special. I like working with animals. You can have a connection with kangaroos, raccoons, or donkeys."

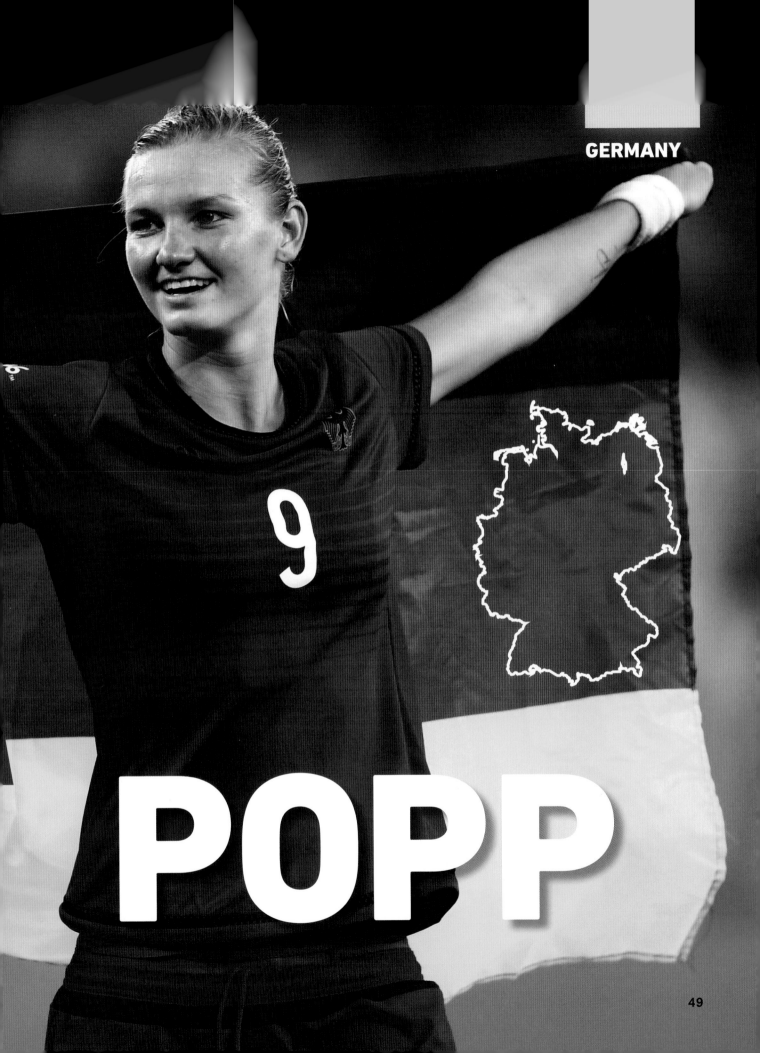

POPP

PUGH

MALLORY PUGH
FORWARD
UNITED STATES
HEIGHT 5 FT 4 IN (162 CM)

BORN APRIL 29, 1998
IN LITTLETON, COLORADO, USA

CURRENT TEAM:
SKY BLUE FC, UNITED STATES

INTERNATIONAL GAMES: 63
GOALS: 18

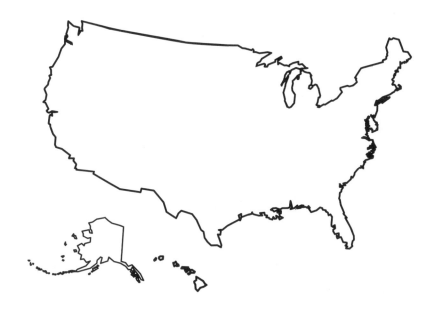

Mallory Pugh was raised with her older sister Brianna in Highlands Ranch, Colorado. Both their parents were competitive runners, and their father also played soccer. Brianna led the way into soccer for their generation. Pugh looked up to her and also started playing soccer at age four. Pugh made the jump to team soccer on Real Colorado in the Colorado Premier League, winning state titles in 2010 and 2011. After a short stint at UCLA, Pugh joined the Washington Spirit in 2017, but transferred in 2020 to Sky Blue FC in New Jersey, where she will be expected to take on a leading role despite her young age. Ever since debuting for Team USA in 2016 and taking part in the Olympics in the same year, Pugh has been a regular on the team, holding her own against much more seasoned stars. Pugh was called up for the 2019 FIFA Women's World Cup and scored her first World Cup goal in the game against Thailand on June 11, 2019. She appeared in all three group stage games against Thailand, Chile, and Sweden, and went on to celebrate her first, but hardly last, World Cup that summer in France.

In 2016, Mia Hamm tweeted of the young prodigy: "Speed kills but technical speed absolutely annihilates defenders. Mallory Pugh is for real." At the time, Pugh was only half a year into her international career. With more than 60 international games behind her already, is Pugh destined to become the greatest player in the world?

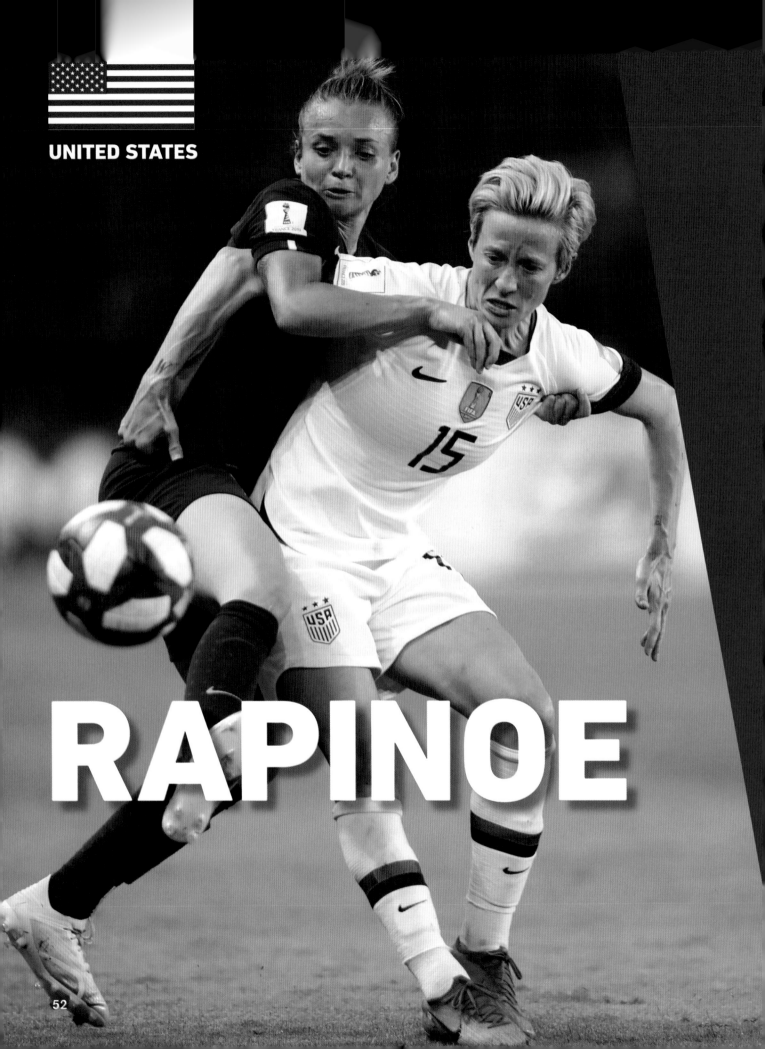

RAPINOE

MEGAN RAPINOE
WINGER
UNITED STATES
HEIGHT 5 FT 6 IN (168 CM)

BORN JULY 5, 1985
REDDING, CALIFORNIA, USA

CURRENT TEAM:
REIGN FC, UNITED STATES

INTERNATIONAL GAMES: 168
GOALS: 52

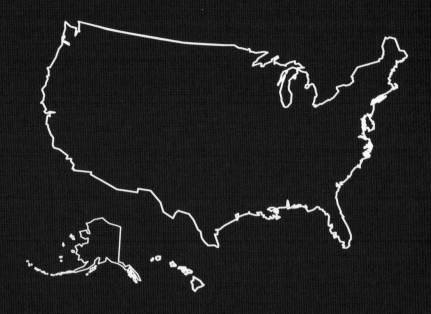

As a player, Megan Rapinoe is always looking to outwit her opponents. It's her agility and dribbling skills, combined with an eye for the goal, that brought her the Golden Boot at the 2019 World Cup. Megan and her fraternal twin Rachael grew up playing soccer together, with Rachael representing the USA at the U-23 level. But it was Megan who, after slow progress in the early years of her career, went on to become the most famous women's soccer player in the world. Her breakout moment came at the age of 28, when she transferred to the all-conquering Olympique Lyonnais in France, where she won the league and the cup. She soon returned to the States and has played for Seattle's Reign FC ever since. Her roster of honors includes two World Cups and one runners-up medal, an Olympic gold, team honors in both France and the United States, and the ultimate individual achievement, the Ballon d'Or, in 2019. But she always emphasizes the collective, as she did when paying tribute to her Team USA teammates after their World Cup victory in 2019: "There is nothing that can faze this group. We're chilling. We've got tea-sipping. We've got celebrations. We've got pink hair and purple hair. We've got tattoos and dreadlocks. We've got white girls and black girls and everything in between. Straight girls and gay girls."

Rapinoe is an outspoken activist. She is an advocate for numerous LGBT organizations and was one of the first white athletes to take a knee in support of the Black Lives Matter movement. Her status as the leader of Team USA has seen her named as one of *Time* magazine's "100 Most Influential People of 2020."

RENARD

WENDIE RENARD
CENTRAL DEFENDER
FRANCE
HEIGHT 6FT 2 IN (188 CM)

BORN JULY 20, 1990
IN SCHŒLCHER, MARTINIQUE

CURRENT TEAM:
OLYMPIQUE LYONNAIS, FRANCE

INTERNATIONAL GAMES: 122
GOALS: 23

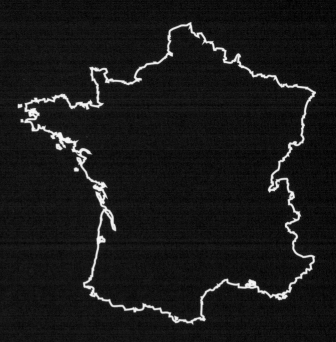

Defenders don't come any more imposing than Wendie Renard. Her towering presence makes her practically unbeatable in the air, while her reading of the game, strength, pace, and technique allow her to thwart most efforts at penetrating the defense. She is also a threat at the other end of the soccer field, scoring plenty from headers and being a proficient set piece taker herself. Renard has gathered a multitude of individual honors (and goals!) from her long and distinguished international career, although the French team has not been able to win major trophies during her time. But it is her long career with Olympique Lyonnais which makes her a legend in the history of soccer. Coinciding with her presence on the team, OL has won an absolutely astounding 14 national championships in a row—which is a unique record in the history of sports. Bearing in mind that Renard is still at the top of her game and nowhere near slowing down, let alone retiring, it is entirely possible that Lyon could reach the milestone of 20 championships in a row. If that transpires, it is impossible to say whether such a record could ever be beaten. And of course, OL has dominated European team competition with Renard as captain—they have won the UEFA Women's Champions League for the last five seasons running.

Renard was born on Martinique, a French island in the Caribbean. When she was 15, she flew to France for a tryout at the national soccer center, Clairefontaine, but was not accepted into the training program. However, when she was 16 she signed professionally with Lyon and has been there since.

CANADA

SINCLAIR

CHRISTINE SINCLAIR
FORWARD
CANADA
HEIGHT 5 FT 9 IN (175 CM)

BORN JUNE 12, 1983
IN BURNABY, BRITISH COLUMBIA, CANADA

CURRENT TEAM:
PORTLAND THORNS FC, USA

NTERNATIONAL GAMES: 296
GOALS: 186

Christine Sinclair serves as captain of the powerful Canadian national team and is the main reason for the team's successes over the last 15 years. She is the true talisman for Canada and the greatest goal scorer that the women's national team has ever seen, netting goals of every possible type. Sinclair is a truly versatile player, capable of shooting with both feet, and along with scoring goals herself, she has a gift for creating opportunities for teammates with precision passes and brilliant playmaking. Asked about Sinclair in a 2014 interview with CBC, the powerful U.S. goalkeeper Hope Solo said: "I've said for a long time that I believe, in my humble opinion, that Christine Sinclair is the best player in the world ... You don't always get to see how brilliant she is because she doesn't always have the support players, but I think now she's starting to get the support players she needs to really highlight her own play." During the 2015 World Cup in Canada, the home team exceeded expectations by making it all the way to the quarterfinals, where they lost by a hair to the stalwart English team. The BBC still raved about Sinclair as a captain who leads by example and inspires her teammates. She was said to be "universally respected by opponents and boasts an international strike rate few can match. Modest and unassuming off the field, Sinclair's drive and passion are hallmarks of her on-field persona."

In 2020, Sinclair has engraved her name into the history of international soccer by surpassing Abby Wambach of the United States as the all-time leading scorer, male or female. She is now up to a staggering 186 goals in international games and still going strong. Will she pass 200?

VAN VEENENDAAL

SARI VAN VEENENDAAL
GOALKEEPER
THE NETHERLANDS
HEIGHT 5 FT 10 IN (178 CM)

BORN APRIL 3, 1990
IN NIEUWEGEIN, THE NETHERLANDS

CURRENT TEAM:
PSV EINDHOVEN, THE NETHERLANDS

INTERNATIONAL GAMES: 68

Sari Van Veenendaal is a product of the Netherlands' proud soccer tradition which gave birth to the system known as "total football." She explains: "I play very much in the Dutch style, playing out from the back—that's how I was always coached. But I can still improve a lot in this respect." After winning everything there was to be won in the Netherlands league system with FC Twente, Van Veenendaal moved to Arsenal, where she was one of a host of Dutch players. Her success continued in London, with three cups won in a span of four years. Since then, she has played in Spain with Atlético Madrid, but is now back home with traditional powerhouse PSV

Eindhoven. Van Veenendaal has established herself as one of the world's best goalkeepers, with the Netherlands winning gold medals at the 2017 Euro and coming in second at the 2019 World Cup, not least due to her inspired efforts. She has been rewarded with a host of individual honors, prime among them her Golden Glove award at the 2019 World Cup, given to the tournament's most outstanding goalkeeper. In the selection for the FIFA FIFpro Women's Team of the Year, Van Veenendaal also won the Best Women's Goalkeeper award, ahead of Chile's Christiane Endler and Sweden's Hedvig Lindahl.

As a mark of her successful career as an athlete, Van Veenendaal has a knighthood! After the UEFA Women's Euro 2017 championship, the whole of the victorious Netherlands team was honored by Prime Minister Mark Rutte and Minister of Sport Edith Schippers and made Knights of the Order of Orange-Nassau.

MARTA

MARTA VIEIRA DA SILVA
FORWARD
BRAZIL
HEIGHT 5 FT 4 IN (162 CM)

BORN FEBRUARY 19, 1986
IN DOIS RIACHOS, ALAGOAS, BRAZIL

CURRENT TEAM:
ORLANDO PRIDE, FLORIDA, USA

INTERNATIONAL GAMES: 154
GOALS: 108

Six-time FIFA World Player of the Year, Marta grew up in a small rural village in central Brazil, but her talents on the field were so conspicuous that major contender Vasco da Gama, based in Rio de Janeiro, invited her to join when she was only 14 years old. Foreign agents soon caught wind of the talented Brazilian, and she set sail on a vast journey. She hasn't looked back since. She played for powerful teams in Sweden and the United States, as well as in Brazil. At only 20, Marta was awarded the first of her six FIFA World Player of Year titles. Marta has been compared to Brazilian geniuses Ronaldo and Ronaldinho, and the legend Pelé even described Marta as a female version of himself. She possesses great speed, precise aim, and scores goals of every possible variety. These skills, with her incredible technique, confident ball control, and superlative dribbling powers, has contributed to Marta earning countless accolades for her talent and goal-scoring achievements. At the team level, Marta has collected national championship trophies with three different squads in Sweden—Umeå IK, Tyresö FF, and FC Rosengård—and two in the States—FC Gold Pride and Western New York Flash—as well as bringing home the Copa Libertadores, South America's premier team competition, with Brazilian Santos.

The Brazilian national team counts among the world's greatest but has had a bumpy ride at World Cup tournaments. Brazil's best performance was at the 2007 World Cup in China where they placed second—mainly due to Marta's genius. She eagerly drove the team, scored seven goals in seven games, and was awarded the Golden Boot.

July 3, 2019: Lieke Martens of the Netherlands and Kosovare Asllani of Sweden during the FIFA Women's World Cup semifinal match in Lyon, France